Praise for

Permission to Slurp

"All too often people get intimidated by the terminology and techniques involved in assessing, evaluating and enjoying quality coffee. Karen explains the whole process so clearly that *Permission to Slurp* will be a major boon to anyone who is interested in learning more about coffee."

– Barry Max Wills, coffee grower in Colombia

"*Permission to Slurp* is a simple yet profound guide that helps both Colombians and foreigners discover our nation's most important product and learn to taste it."

– Luís Fernando Vélez, owner of Amor Perfecto Café

"Colombia is the place to be for coffee, and *Permission to Slurp* will walk you through everything you need to know about the world of specialty coffee. This book teaches you the basics so that you can make the most of Bogota's coffee scene."

– Stephany Moore, CEO, Social Coffee House

"Thanks to *Permission to Slurp* I've discovered underground coffee shops all over Bogota and upgraded both my morning coffee preparation routine and the beans that go into it. *Permission to Slurp* is friendly and encouraging – it's impossible not to get caught up in the author's passion for Colombian coffee and the people whose lives depend on it."
– Victoria Kellaway, author of *Colombia a Comedy of Errors*

"*Permission to Slurp* is the result of Karen's own coffee journey: many hours spent in conversation with baristas, roasters, growers and café owners, and many many cups of coffee. It is both a straightforward guide book to the sometimes intimidating world of specialty coffee, and a tribute to the many Colombians who earn their living from this marvelous bean."

– Suzie Hoban, Lecturer in Cacao and Coffee (University of La Sabana)

"With *Permission to Slurp*, a fearless Karen Attman is boldly forming a new generation of coffee snobs! For her tireless work in making us aware of the value of good coffee, we should all be grateful. Beware baristas, I'm coming for you and Attman is to blame."

– Richard McColl, host of Colombia Calling radio show

"The treasure map to understanding and finding Colombian specialty coffee is written within the pages of Karen Attman's book, *Permission to Slurp*. And as you dive into the world of specialty coffee, everyone in the industry will give you permission to slurp."

– Lisa Brayda, head barista and manager at Art Café, New York

Permission to Slurp

The Insider's Guide to Tasting
Specialty Coffee in Colombia

Karen Attman

BOGOTÁ INTERNATIONAL PRESS

This book is dedicated to all the baristas, both in Colombia and around the world, who believe that specialty coffee changes lives.

Through their passion for outstanding coffee, commitment to supporting farming communities, and hard work in passing their dedication on to consumers, these baristas help improve the lives of people all along the coffee chain.

Permission to Slurp

Contents

Contents

Searching for a Treasure

A treasure hunt is taking place in Colombia. While the treasure does have monetary value for some, its true worth is far greater than just a healthy bank account.

Do you want to come along on the hunt? You'll need to be well-equipped. As with any treasure hunt, to find the buried gold you need to 1) know what the treasure is, 2) have access to the map that shows where to locate the treasure, and 3) find where X marks the spot.

So, the first step. What is this treasure? Specialty coffee. Uncovering the best coffee is part of a discovery process that leads you to outstanding flavors and aromas. You'll not only find the coffees that enrich your morning routine and enliven your afternoons. No, specialty coffee is more than that. Specialty coffee takes you on a journey around the world and into the lives of hundreds of thousands of coffee farmers. Sound cool? It is.

However, it gets even better. You see, there's a treasure within a treasure. The deeper and richer treasure embedded within Colombian specialty coffee is hope.

Perhaps you've heard that Colombia has been afflicted with an internal conflict that has lasted almost six decades. The amount of pain and loss that people have been subjected to is incomprehensible.

However, beyond the pain lies the hope of rebirth, of creating a path towards peace and healing. At this crucial time in Colombia's history, when a historic peace agreement was signed between the government and a major player in the conflict (November 2016), many factors come together to help make that hope of a better future a reality.

Coffee is one of those factors. It is tightly wrapped up in Colombia's past and is linked to the collective dream that millions of people have of building a better future.

Coffee plays a part in the dream that hundreds of thousands of displaced villagers and farmers have. These are people who simply aspire to live in peace; in many cases they want to return home, discover new opportunities and revive old ones, and provide for their families.

Although the journey will be long, specialty coffee is one of the many ways people can advance along that path. A farmer who produces specialty coffee can attract buyers who work directly with individual farmers rather than co-ops, where coffee is often blended together regardless of the quality.

Eliminating the middleman translates into higher profits for the producer. Higher profits mean a better standard of living for small coffee farmers. In fact, specialty coffee can improve people's lives in every step of the coffee chain – farmers, pickers, tasters, and baristas.

So now you know what this double treasure is. How do you get access to the map?

We've made it easy for you. This book is the map that leads you to the treasure. With it we'll take you on a journey around Colombia to discover what makes a coffee special, what contributes to producing the best coffees, and how these coffees are processed (in simple terms). We'll peek into a few of the challenges coffee farmers face.

And along the way you'll learn to select, brew and taste these specialty coffees, a super power you can take with you wherever you live or wherever you travel around the world.

Let's start the adventure.

Chapter 1

The Truth about Specialty Coffee

Defining the best

In Colombia I hear the same phrase over and over again: Colombian coffee is the best. Of course, when Colombians are the ones stating that, you might have some doubts about their impartiality on the subject. As I heard it repeated again and again, I asked myself the inevitable question: "Is Colombian coffee really superior?"

However, Colombians aren't the only ones who affirm that their beans are better. Growing up in the United States, I heard about Colombian coffee my whole life.

I had seen Juan Valdez ads on TV where the moustached coffee farmer appeared with his mule Conchita to persuade people to choose Colombian coffee over the (apparently) inferior competition. I had often seen the little seal on coffee bags that proudly boasted 100% Colombian coffee.

From childhood it was burned into my brain: Colombian coffee is the best.

Granted, without a doubt this had to do with the excellent marketing plan concocted by the Colombian Coffee Growers Federation. But we know that fancy ad campaigns and bright-colored seals and awards don't guarantee a superior product.

In fact, since the Juan Valdez brand was at one time closely associated with supermarket coffees – hardly a specialty or 'gourmet' coffee line – it might seem to not be that special of a coffee after all.

When major publications in the United States and Europe commissioned me to write articles about Colombian coffee, I began to question the statement that I had heard since childhood.

So I began to investigate that topic: Is there any reason to believe that Colombia produces better coffee than other countries? And if so, why?

I was amazed (and as a food writer living in Colombia, enormously pleased) to find that Colombia does in fact have reasons to boast about producing some of the best coffee in the world. That's what this book is about.

Although I could go on for hours – and fill several books – about the reasons, I don't want to give you coffee overload. This book will briefly give you the tools you'll need to discover the best coffees and prepare them at home.

So to make a complicated subject easy, I'm going to break it down for you in brief sections that will guide you both as you discover coffee in Colombia and as you taste specialty coffee at home.

What is specialty coffee?

Since this book is a guide to tasting specialty coffees, let's define what specialty coffee is and how you can recognize it.

Basically, coffee earns the title of specialty when it is grown and processed according to strict quality controls. It is the end result of careful cultivation, processing, roasting and brewing.

A coffee farmer who wants to produce specialty coffee starts by carefully selecting the variety, or the type of plant, that will best grow in the specific climate and soil conditions on a particular farm. The plant is cultivated according to its particular requirements for years until it begins to produce enough fruit to be commercially viable.

From there, the fruit and bean have to be processed in specific ways and handled with care up to the point of reaching the roaster. The roaster, in turn, determines the optimum roast that will make the characteristics of the coffee shine.

The journey does not stop when the bean is roasted and shipped to a coffee shop. Those amazing flavor profiles can only be appreciated when the beverage is prepared in a way that brings out its best qualities. That involves the work of talented baristas who understand each coffee and dedicate the time to brew it right. Any mistakes along the path can lead to an inferior coffee.

Why go to all that trouble? Because when it's done right, this path leads to unique coffees with flavor profiles that can dazzle your palate.

At this point you may be asking yourself a valid question: Can a coffee shop just slap a specialty coffee label on anything, regardless of quality? No. At least, they shouldn't.

True specialty coffee is graded by professional cuppers on a scale of 1-100, and the goal of any self-respecting specialty coffee is to score as high as possible.

It's like being back in school – you always hope for a perfect grade (or at least a passing one). For coffee, a score above 80 is that passing grade, the number that puts it into the specialty category. We'll discuss this grading system in detail in Chapter 4.

It costs *how much*?

But isn't specialty coffee more expensive? Yes, it is. Just like a fine wine is a world apart in price – and taste – from a lifeless wine in a cardboard box, specialty coffee generally comes with a higher price tag. In fact, in this book we'll talk about numerous similarities between fine wine and specialty coffee.

This elevated price makes sense. Why?

A coffee farmer who wants to produce specialty coffee has worked hard to cultivate the highest quality beans using the best processes. He or she gave those plants the care that is often reserved for a newborn child. The coffee cherries were picked with care and meticulously processed. A good roaster, who has perfected the craft over years of intense study and practice, has roasted the beans according to a specific recipe to achieve optimal results.

Those beans were packaged in special bags to protect the quality. The coffee shop owner diligently handled the bags. A barista lovingly took extra time to prepare the best brew possible.

Yes, all of that care means the coffee will be more expensive.

Compared to the price of craft beers or a high quality chocolate, that bag of specialty coffee doesn't seem so expensive. In fact, when you see the prices in Colombia for a pound of extraordinary coffee or a labor-intensive pour-over brew prepared by a true coffee expert, you'll be astounded at how cheap it all comes.

Now we come to the question that still hangs in the air: Is specialty coffee worth the price? That's a question each coffee drinker has to answer for themselves. We could affirm that beauty is in the eye of the beholder and flavor is in the palate of the taster. So what one person considers expensive, another person could consider reasonable.

No doubt, if you're reading this book it's because the hunt for outstanding coffee thrills you. You delight in the aromas and flavors and that feeling of satisfaction that a perfect cup of coffee gives you. That satisfaction is worth the slightly elevated price.

You're certainly not alone in that search. The specialty coffee industry has been rapidly growing, to the point that in the United States it has reached 55% of the market share in the coffee industry. Many consumers recognize the value of true specialty coffee and are willing to pay a bit more for a higher quality coffee.

Two major players

Let's go back to a basic question about specialty coffee, the point where it all begins. What does specialty coffee start with?

It all begins with the type of plant or tree (the two terms are correct). You may be amazed to learn there are about 100 species of coffee plants, with thousands of varieties!

However, don't get coffee overwhelm thinking about all those differences. There are just two species of coffee plants that are used commercially around the world, and from them we get a handful of varieties. Most specialty coffee comes from just one particular species of coffee plant.

In fact, in Colombia farmers only plant that one species. To understand why, we'll talk about both of those commercially viable species. Let me introduce them to you.

One is an attractive, sophisticated type (think James Bond) and the other is his less appreciated brother. Their names are Arabica and Robusta.

Let's first talk about the ugly duckling, Robusta.

Robusta is known for its generally harsh, bitter taste and disappointing flavors. This is partially because the bean has less sugar and lipids and is higher in caffeine (which is bitter) than Arabica. At times this is also due to poor harvesting techniques, which we'll talk about later.

Although there are Robusta beans that break the mold and produce a superior coffee, in general you're not going to be impressed with its spectacular flavor profiles.

Since the Robusta bean is generally lower quality, why would farmers choose to grow it?

The simple reason is because the plant is more resistant to disease and grows at lower elevations, which makes it easier to cultivate and harvest. This also means that Robusta is significantly cheaper than most Arabica varieties. Robusta often lurks in coffee blends and instant coffees.

Meanwhile, Robusta's handsome brother, Arabica, is highly prized around the world (can you hear the Bond music playing softly in the background?). This species generally produces a better quality bean and sweet, bright, aromatic coffees.

Colombia only cultivates Arabica coffee, which is one of the reasons coffee experts come to Colombia to find the best beans. The rest of this book (which is, after all, about Colombian coffee) will only discuss Arabica.

Why so many varieties?

As I mentioned, coffee comes in many varieties. This can sound confusing, but to make it easier let's think of something you may know well – apples.

Perhaps you like apples in general, though you may love a certain variety of apple. Maybe what thrills you is the sweetness of a Red Delicious or the crisp tartness of a Granny Smith.

Similarly, coffee has many varieties, each with their particular characteristics.

In Colombia you'll find many varieties of Arabica coffee. Each variety best adapts to different growing conditions – including rainfall, shade, soil and temperature – and farmers choose the coffee variety that is best suited to the conditions on their farm.

Additionally, every variety has a different flavor profile. Of course, you have to try many coffees to get to the point of tasting one and saying, "Ah, what an excellent example of a Yellow Bourbon!"

While that might sound farfetched, it's not. It's similar to a wine connoisseur recognizing and marveling over an excellent Pinot Noir.

Naturally, an expert can only achieve that level after trying many, many glasses of wine. So take heart – with time and practice you can also learn to appreciate the subtleties of coffee varieties.

So let's briefly go over some of the varieties you'll see in Colombia. You'll be able to put this knowledge into practice when you visit specialty coffee shops, since the variety of the bean is marked on packages of single estate coffees (coffees from just one farm).

Common coffee varieties in Colombia

Typica

This was the first variety introduced to most countries where coffee is now grown. About 25% of coffee trees in Colombia are Typica. It has a lower yield than other coffee varieties but produces a sweet and clean cup.

Castillo

This highly productive variety was developed in Colombia. Castillo is suitable for local conditions, since it is resistant to common diseases that threaten coffee crops throughout the Americas. It also produces a consistently good quality coffee.

Caturra

This one arrived in Colombia from Brazil. Ripe cherries can be red or yellow and the plant grows low to the ground, making it easier to harvest. Caturra is highly productive and the coffee trees can be planted close together.

About 45% of the coffee grown in Colombia is this variety. It is generally considered to produce coffees with delicate body and bright acidity, and it is not as sweet as other varieties.

Colombia

Yes, this variety was named after the country, since it was developed here in the 1980s. It's very productive and resistant to disease. It often has notes of panela, a type of raw sugar, and chocolate, which are both characteristic of Colombian coffees.

Bourbon

This one came to the Americas by means of an island once known as Bourbon (now called Réunion Island). The cherries, which can be red, yellow or orange, are smaller but the plant produces more cherries than Typica. Higher acidity is nicely balanced out by a distinctive sweetness in a bean that is fragrant, complex, and delicate.

Geisha

Originally from a town in Ethiopia called Gesha, this variety went through a name change when it moved to the Americas.

Geisha has been grown in Central America for decades but only recently captured attention as a complex coffee that has won its share of prizes at competitions and high prices per pound.

Although it is not a common variety in Colombia, Geisha is slowly gaining in popularity. Some love its delicate floral notes, while others find the lighter body disappointing.

Part of the excitement when visiting a specialty coffee shop is that the available coffees can change from day to day according to harvests, climate, and other variables. You will never know what delights you'll get in your cup, so relish the unexpected discoveries and the opportunity to try many varieties.

Get out the map

Naturally, geography plays an important role in coffee cultivation. In fact, the specific area where a coffee is grown can have a profound effect on how the beans taste. All coffee is cultivated in what is known as the Coffee Belt or the Bean Belt, which is a band swaddling the globe near the equator.

The ideal growing conditions for Arabica extend from about 3,000 feet to 7,000 feet (920 to 2133 meters) above sea level.

Perhaps you'd never think that altitude would change the flavors in your coffee cup, but it does. A cooler mountain climate means the beans take longer to mature. This is when they develop more complex sugars that produce intense floral, berry, and citrus flavors in the cup.

Keeping that in mind, it's easy to see why Arabica coffee grows well in Colombia, since the country has an abundance of mountains. The Andes Mountains dissect the country from north to south and branch out in three parallel mountain ranges.

These mountains not only provide the conditions we mentioned above, but they are also home to an estimated one sixth of the world's plant species – all this in a relatively small area.

Yes, coffee in Colombia is grown in some of the most biologically diverse areas in the world. Additionally, much of the soil in Colombia's coffee growing regions is well-drained volcanic soil, and the high organic content produces an excellent coffee.

How much rain falls – and when – also affects the quality of coffee. Arabica prefers pleasant weather year-round (60-70°F or 15-21°C) with regular rainfall and adequate sunshine. Partial shade improves coffee, and in Colombia the majority of coffee farms are partially shaded.

Around the world, coffee plants generally produce one harvest a year. However, Colombia breaks that rule. Alternating wet and dry seasons create a second coffee harvest, or *mitaca*, in some areas of the country. In some very specific microclimates there is even a third coffee harvest. That's good news for lovers of Colombian coffee – you'll be able to get fresh beans throughout the year.

As we can see, much of Colombia's geography meets the rather picky requirements of Arabica coffee trees.

Wherever you travel around the country, from north to south and east to west, you'll discover suitable geography for Arabica coffee production. And conditions such as temperature, altitude, soil, and rain patterns give Colombian coffees rich flavor, full body, and balanced acidity.

So while we can say that excellent specialty coffees are produced in many countries around the world, specific characteristics in Colombia truly do make it possible to produce large amounts of higher quality coffee.

Meet the Experts

Back in the 1990s – when almost no one in Colombia was interested in roasting specialty coffee – Luis Fernando Vélez had the vision of providing superior coffee that would stay in the country. He worked with coffee farmers to discover coffees that surpassed the current expectations.

His flagship store in Bogota has a coffee lab and training area where baristas learn to hone their craft. His coffee brand, Amor Perfecto, is sold in over 600 establishments around the country and has changed the way many Colombians drink coffee.

Chapter 2

Coffee Culture in Colombia

How Colombians brew coffee

Colombians typically start their morning with a *tinto*. It's generally a small cup of black coffee, often heavily sweetened with sugar or panela. In Bogota, you can find people selling tinto on nearly every street corner and in every bakery.

Later in the day Colombians will drink *café*, which is coffee with milk (typically lots of milk and just a hint of coffee). If you're going to order a coffee in Colombia, remember to ask for a tinto or an *americano* if you want black coffee, and a café if you want your coffee drowned in milk.

In some homes, coffee is made using a cloth filter hung on a circular wire. The cloth filter, which is internationally called a coffee sock because of its resemblance to the article of clothing, gets a dose of coffee grinds and then boiling water is poured over.

One of the drawbacks to this brewing method is that the thick cloth doesn't allow the oils in coffee to pass through, which negatively affects the flavor. The fabric is also difficult to clean, and at times it isn't changed for weeks (or months) and can get quite dark and crusty.

Another common way to make coffee doesn't have a name, but it's often used on farms. I got to see it expertly brewed when I visited a Colombian grandmother. She put an aluminum pot filled with water on the stove and heated it to boiling. She threw in the coffee grinds and let them boil for a while, and then she removed the pot from the heat.

She watched the brew intently until the grinds sank to the bottom, then carefully poured off the coffee without using a filter. In the United States this is called cowboy coffee. So how did this Colombian cowboy coffee taste? I have to say, it was much better than I thought it would be – I think she threw a dose of grandmotherly love into that pot.

In some areas of Colombia Moka coffee pots are used. Popular in Italy, they are considered mini stovetop espresso makers (which they are not). You'll see Moka coffee pots in supermarkets in Colombia. I owned one for a long time, and I like how easy it is to use and clean.

Sometimes coffee is made in the morning, left in an aluminum pot on the back of the stove, and is reheated throughout the day whenever someone needs a caffeine kick.

Another popular custom, especially in hot areas of the country, is to use instant coffee. No comments on that one.

A sad reality about the coffee Colombians drink is that it is often the worst quality coffee.

In fact, coffee consumed here might not even be from Colombia. At times cheaper, inferior coffee is imported from neighboring countries and mixed in the blends. This creates a cheaper product, and low price is often the determining factor when Colombians decide which coffee to purchase.

How much coffee do they drink?

How much coffee do you drink in a year? Have you ever considered that how much you drink may depend on where you're from?

Total coffee consumption in the world amounted to over 150 million bags from October 2015 to September 2016. And those aren't the one pound bags you buy at your coffee shop. We're talking about 60 kg (132 lb.) sacks, which is how green coffee is sold.

The European Union imports 45% of all coffee exports, which makes that region the largest coffee importer. In 2013 their imports totaled over 3 million metric tons of coffee, or over 51 million sacks.

All those figures sound pretty dry, but from them a fun annual per capita consumption rate can be calculated. Keep in mind that these calculations are based on everyone in the country, including children and others who don't drink coffee.

Not surprisingly given the import figures, Europe has the highest per capita coffee consumption in the world. On average, every resident of the European Union consumes 4 kilos (8.8 lbs.) of roasted beans per year, which is just under 2 cups of coffee every day.

That's a little higher than the average person in the United States. However, some countries blow that statistic out of the water.

- Brazil 4.8 kg (10.5 lbs.)
- Germany 5.2 kg (11.4 lbs.)
- Netherlands 6.7 kg (15 lbs.)
- Norway 7.2 kg (15.8 lbs.)
- Finland gulps down 9.6 kg (21 lbs.) per person

And Colombia? The average consumption per person in a recent year was just 2 kg (4.4 lbs.). And that's an increase from previous years!

Does that surprise you? Actually, some coffee producing countries, such as Costa Rica and Guatemala, drink a sixth of that.

Why so little? While it is true that Colombians in general drink coffee several times a day, the coffee tends to be a small cups of weak tinto or a mug of milk with a touch of coffee in it, which doesn't do much to budge the national consumption levels.

So it's not surprising that while in 2015 Colombia produced 14.2 million sacks of coffee (those 60 kg behemoths), they left only 1.5 million sacks in the country for internal consumption.

The chart below shows per capita coffee consumption averages for several European countries and contrasts that with the per capita consumption in Colombia.

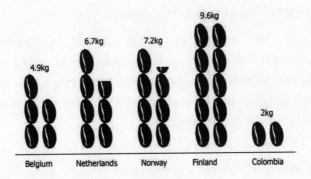

Statistics from Euromonitor, 2013

When did coffee arrive in Colombia?

Coffee embarked on a long journey before it found its way to Colombia. Discovered about 1,000 years ago in Ethiopia, coffee began to be shipped to Europe in the early 1600s. Coffee houses began to become popular in major European cities in the mid-1600s. Then coffee took off as a common drink around the world, and it began to be cultivated in tropical areas outside of Africa. By the early 1700s it was being cultivated in Central America.

The exact date coffee arrived in Colombia is unknown, but it seems to have landed in the early 1700s. At that time Colombia had other important crops such as sugar and bananas, but by the late 1800s coffee was a dominant crop, especially for export.

At that time most land then was owned by large landowners, which concentrated wealth in just a few pockets. Land reforms in Colombia mean that now most coffee farms are small. Fast forwarding to modern times, 2.3 million acres of land in Colombia are now planted with coffee.

In the 1960s coffee accounted for almost 90% of all exports from Colombia. Although that figure is much lower now, coffee is still the most important export after oil and mining, and coffee is still Colombia's primary agricultural export.

Who runs coffee farms? In some countries, large corporations generally own and operate immense farms.

However, in Colombia the vast majority of coffee farms (95%) are operated by families. Coffee in Colombia is typically grown on small farms that are generally no more than five acres. So Colombian coffee is about Colombian families, and purchasing coffee here directly affects their quality of life.

Around the country more than 555,000 families are involved in growing coffee, and what they produce made up 16% of the national agricultural GDP in 2010.

In fact, 2.4 million Colombians (25% of the rural population) depend on coffee production. About 2.5 acres of land planted with coffee provides a Colombian family with the equivalent of one month's minimum salary.

This long history of coffee farming has produced not only excellent coffee, but also a traditional lifestyle that stretches back for generations.

At times when we think of coffee culture, upscale city dwellers downing expensive brews may pop into our minds. However, coffee in Colombia has been an integral part of the national culture for hundreds of years, creating regional traditions that revolve around the precious bean.

Those traditional lifestyles in some coffee growing regions are so particular that UNESCO includes one of them in the World Heritage List. In that region, which is called Colombia's coffee growing axis or triangle (*eje cafetero*), small towns and villages have remained unchanged for many decades in a lifestyle that has been passed down from one generation to another.

Whole communities in these regions are dedicated to coffee production, and they have developed innovative systems to manage natural resources. Literally everyone in the family may be involved in cultivating coffee, from grandma all the way down to young children.

They've also developed particular foods, traditions, festivals, clothing and architecture. So a farmer in that region may take his harvest to town atop a colorful Jeep Willy while his wife makes what is nationally known as *bandeja paisa* for lunch. A worker may rake coffee several times a day over a cement patio outside the farmhouse. The whole family enjoys numerous coffee-related festivals throughout the year.

Even though fluctuating prices can create crisis in the industry, coffee production continues to be an important source of employment in rural regions. You can see that coffee is an integral part of Colombian identity.

Should you care what region a coffee comes from?

When you listen to coffee experts in Colombia talk about specialty coffee, you'll hear them mention regions over and over again. What are those regions?

Regions are simply where the coffee is grown. You'll see the names of the region or department (state or province) on the bags of specialty coffees you buy. Some names you'll see frequently are: Quindío, Cundinamarca, Tolima, Huila, Santander, Magdalena, Antioquia, Caldas, and Nariño.

Why should you care what region the coffee was grown in? To answer that, let's return to wine. Should a wine connoisseur care where a wine is from?

Isn't it true that wine from Rioja, Spain, tastes different than a wine from Bordeaux, France or one from Napa Valley in California? The terroir (a fancy-sounding term meaning the land, soil, and climate where the grapes are grown) affects the final tastes. Additionally, each area may have distinct wine-making traditions.

Not surprisingly, growing coffee is similar to growing grapes: different areas produce different tastes. Each region in Colombia produces coffee that has slightly different taste profiles. Conditions that we've mentioned, such as altitude, rainfall, shade and sun, change the tastes you get in the cup.

So some areas produce coffee with more body, some with more acidity, some that are sweeter, others that are nutty. Colombian coffee can have rich chocolate tones or light fruity notes – and everything in between.

What are single estate coffees?

Many specialty coffees will talk about the origin, or the farm the coffee is from (*origen* in Spanish). Labeled as single estate coffees, they are generally more expensive. However, does it really matter what farm the coffee was grown on?

In a word, yes.

If the coffee producer has worked tirelessly to give the coffee plants the necessary care to ensure a higher quality bean and has been meticulous in harvesting and processing that bean, the result will be an excellent coffee. So you can look for coffee from that particular farm and consistently expect the best, just like you can expect a certain quality wine from a specific vineyard.

Knowing which farm has produced what coffee not only benefits the consumer, but also benefits the coffee farmer, the workers, and ultimately the whole country. Why?

If the farmer has worked hard to produce an excellent specialty coffee, they will receive better prices for each harvest. That impels them to strive towards excellence in harvesting, processing and transport. How workers on the farm are being treated can also be traced. For instance, are their wages considered fair for the region?

Lastly, it also means that a farm's impact on the environment can be measured. Deforestation and pollution are environmental problems in Colombia, and sustainable coffee production can help mitigate these conditions through well-managed and responsible farming.

Meet the Experts

Formed 15 years ago, InConexus is a direct trade export company with its heart set on helping farmers at a local level. Co-founders Carlos Torres and Adriana Villanueva work to connect Colombian farmers with coffee exporters and buyers in other countries.

However, their interest doesn't stop there. They also coordinate assistance to improve infrastructure in rural areas, help farmers develop sustainable practices, negotiate higher prices for green coffee, and participate in other programs that benefit more than 10,000 coffee farmers.

Chapter 3

The Incredible Journey from Plant to Cup

A flower, a fruit and a seed

When talking about this plant to cup journey, the obvious star of the show is the bean. However, have you ever stopped to think about those beans hiding in the coffee bags in your kitchen cabinet? What are they? Are they really beans? Like a kidney bean? Or are they manufactured, like a jelly bean? In fact, they are neither one nor the other.

A coffee bean is a seed from a fruit. If this is hard to imagine, think of a peach. Inside that sweet, ripe fruit lurks a pit, which is the seed. As you know, if you plant that seed in the ground, at some point it will produce a tree.

Coffee plants are quite similar; they produce a fruit and inside that fruit is a seed. In the case of coffee, the seed is a double one, where the flat sides face each other inside the fruit.

Of course, the difference between coffee and peach pits is that human beings found out that if they process the coffee seed, roast it, grind it and add water, they get an irresistible beverage. That seed is what is sold in the coffee bag that you buy at the supermarket or your local coffee shop.

The fruit on the coffee plant is called a cherry. It's a fitting name, since it's rather small and round and quite often red when it's ripe. Yes, it can be eaten, and as you may guess, it does have a fruity flavor.

Friends of mine in coffee growing areas have told me they don't think twice about popping a coffee cherry into their mouths to enjoy the tart fruit, spitting out the seed. In some areas it's considered the poor man's candy, since it's a readily available sweet treat.

For now, let's back up a bit. Months before there was even a seed, there was a flower. Coffee blossoms are delicate, white flowers with an enchanting scent of jasmine. Arabica is self-pollinating, so the flowers always result in fruit.

Going back even further, before there was a flower the coffee tree spent about 3-5 years growing before it was mature enough to produce beans for commercial use. A coffee plant will continue to be productive until it's about 20 years old. After that it can still live on for decades, but since production is usually low the plants are generally not used commercially.

However, how does the coffee seed wind up in the bag you bought at the store? What coffee farmers do to prepare it for drinking is an incredible and complex journey. Let's start with getting the cherries off the plant.

Meet the Experts

When Mauricio Romero, Colombia's national barista champion in 2015, chose his coffee for the world barista championships, he didn't choose a young coffee plant.

He sought out coffee from thirty year-old trees, whose deep root system brought up all the hidden nutrients that created a fascinating, complex, sweet coffee. However, those older plants aren't commercially viable, which is why you can't buy Mauricio's stellar coffee in any shop.

Who harvests coffee?

In many countries, coffee (especially Robusta coffee) is grown on flat stretches of land at sea level where machines can harvest huge amounts of cherries in a short space of time.

That could sound positive, but take a moment to think about it.

Not all cherries on a coffee tree ripen at the same time. Therefore, during harvest time each tree will have both ripe and unripe cherries. A machine can't tell the difference between a cherry that's ready to be picked and one that still needs a couple of weeks to reach its peak. Just imagine how bitter and repulsive coffee made from unripe cherries would taste.

So machine-picked coffee has everything thrown in, both the desirable and the undesirable. That includes cherries at all stages of ripeness as well as twigs and leaves. The idea is that these should be picked out before processing the coffee.

In contrast, how is coffee picked in Colombia? We already mentioned that in Colombia the coffee farms are in the mountains, and all those coffee plants growing on steep slopes can't be harvested using machines.

That's why coffee in Colombia is mostly picked by hand. Obviously, manual picking contributes to a superior coffee. As we mentioned, a machine can't distinguish between an almost ripe or overripe cherry, but a human being can. In fact, the care taken during harvesting can be a major factor in determining the quality of coffee.

There's no doubt that harvesting by hand requires immense amounts of labor, which provides jobs for people in rural communities where there are few other work opportunities. However, coffee harvesting remains a low-paying job that many rural workers avoid. Coffee farmers face the constant challenge of getting their coffee picked while at the same time keeping costs low enough to operate the farm.

How is the fruit removed?

Once the cherries are picked, the first order of business for farmers is to get the seed out of the fruit. To do that, as soon as the coffee cherry is harvested it goes through a series of steps to remove the fruit. There are two basic ways to do this: the washed process and the natural (dry) process.

The washed process

In the washed process, the cherries first go through a pulping machine that removes the bulk of the fruit. However, there is still a final layer that needs to be removed. It's actually very hard to remove that final layer, called mucilage, from the seed, since it sticks tenaciously to the bean. If it's not all removed, flavor defects could creep in. No one wants an odd-tasting coffee, so farmers know the importance of removing the mucilage.

Thankfully, someone discovered that natural enzymes can dissolve this layer, and those enzymes get to work in water. That's why coffee growers soak the beans for a fermentation period that can last from 12 hours to 2 days, or even more.

This is one of those crucial moments in coffee production – if it's done badly, the coffee will taste sour. Done right, the washed process leaves the coffee with clean, bright, fruity tastes. In Colombia coffee farmers normally use the washed processes to remove the fruit, which is one of the factors that makes Colombian coffee superior.

Dried and ready

After their bath, the beans have to be dried to about 10-12% moisture content. In Colombia this is usually done by sun drying; the coffee is spread out on level surfaces such as concrete or raised beds and repeatedly raked about every 6 hours until it dries. The beans can also be machine dried.

This process is important; if the beans are not dried enough, just imagine the bacteria that could grow! On the other hand, beans that are over-dried are brittle and can break during shipping.

But what about the natural (dry) process?

There's another way to process the cherry: the natural or dry process. This is the oldest way of processing coffee and is especially common in countries where there is little water or rainfall. After harvest, the whole cherry is simply placed in the sun to dry, which can take up to a month.

It could be roughly compared to drying a grape into a raisin, although in coffee the dried fruit is later removed. This process can add flavors to coffee, such as berry or tropical fruit flavors. However, it can add unpleasant flavors such as a woody plant taste. So some experts love natural processed coffees, but many shy away from them.

Obviously, this method isn't practical in rainy or damp climates, where the coffee would ferment before it dried.

After drying, the beans are hulled to remove a thin layer called parchment. Then they are sorted. Coffee beans with defects are rejected at this step.

Then they are ready to be shipped to where they will be roasted. This could be done at the farm, at a nearby roaster owned by a cooperative, in a nearby city, or a far-away country. That next step in the journey is the roasting process. This is a key step for specialty coffees.

Meet the Experts

Manuel Torres wants to see all coffee farmers get a fair price for their coffee. He travels by bus to farms in the coffee region just outside of Bogota and works out deals directly with farmers.

At times he brings his 60 kg sack of coffee back on his lap, since coffee can't be stored in the cargo area. If you're in Bogota, try to time a visit to his Contraste Coffee Lab right after he's roasted a batch of coffee.

How dark should you go?

What type of roast do you like? This is an important question, since roasting greatly affects flavor. How the coffee is roasted affects acidity, bitterness, body, and sweetness.

The degree of the roast comes from applying a certain amount of heat to the bean for a determined length of time to provoke a whole range of chemical reactions. Roasts vary from light to very dark, and can produce everything from a smooth and mild coffee to a bright coffee with complex flavors to a dark, heavy cup.

Light roasts tend to have pronounced acidity. A very dark roast lowers acidity, which could sound positive. However, dark roasts may also mask any specific characteristics the bean has.

So a bean that could have produced a bright and flavorful coffee may be transformed into a disappointingly dull one if it is roasted too dark. The goal of a good roaster should be to highlight the special characteristics of a particular coffee.

Which roast is better? Really, roast preferences ultimately depend on the tastes of the one drinking the brew. Dark roasts are common in the United States and parts of Europe. However, in Colombia you'll mainly find lighter roasts. Why?

As mentioned, in Colombia most coffee is grown at higher altitudes, which means the beans have developed complex flavors.

So perhaps your coffee will taste like berries. Or it will have a refreshing touch of lemon. Or a hint of grapes. You may find delicate notes of orange blossoms. Or you may detect a satisfying hazelnut aftertaste.

If the beans are roasted too dark, all those flavors will be covered up. Gone. Disappeared.

Therefore, when you taste coffees in Colombia, be prepared for a lighter roast, a light-colored brew, and more delicate body.

We've now reached an exciting moment in our plant-to-cup journey: the coffee in *your* cup.

Meet the Experts

Jaime Duque, a dedicated agronomist, worked with the Colombian Coffee Growers Federation for nearly two decades. He recently shifted his attention to share his deep knowledge of coffee and coffee science at his coffee shop, Catación Pública.

As a roaster he has the unusual goal of single-handedly roasting beans from every coffee growing region around the country. He believes deeply in education as a force for change, and works with coffee farmers as well as consumers to promote Colombian coffee both within the country and abroad.

Chapter 4

How to Cup Coffee like a Pro

The road to excellence

What is coffee cupping? Different from just sitting down to enjoy a coffee at your favorite coffeehouse, coffee cupping (or tasting) is serious business.

Coffee cupping is the professional process that *defines the overall quality of a particular coffee.*

Cupping is essential for coffee companies. You can imagine a coffee buyer heading off to a far-away country to purchase coffee. How do they know which coffees to buy? Should they just believe the coffee grower or coffee association that a particular coffee is outstanding? No, they have to try it for themselves to see if the coffee fits in with what their customers want.

Cupping is also essential to coffee farmers. When a coffee is judged to be superior, a farmer can demand – and receive – higher prices.

Generally, many coffees are cupped, or tasted, at a single session. Coffee cupping often involves comparing coffees from within a single region, but several regions or countries can also be cupped in one session.

This is no easy task. Distinguishing specific characteristics in each cup when you are simultaneously being impacted by many aromas and flavors can be overwhelming. Additionally, each person has different expectations of what constitutes an excellent coffee.

Your personal journey into the world of cupping specialty coffee, however, should simply be fun. Although professionals follow strict rules during the cupping process – after all, their work and reputation depend on it – we can just relax and have a good time.

Taking a look at what the professionals do can take your coffee appreciation to a deeper level. Once you learn how to judge a coffee, you open the door to developing the ability to detect the finer characteristics of coffee.

On the other hand, that knowledge should never restrict you or take away your joy of discovery. You don't want to be so intent on defining the characteristics of a coffee that you don't enjoy the brew.

I get a thrill of excitement when I go to a specialty coffee house, breathe in the fragrance of freshly ground beans, then sip the brewed coffee slowly and purposefully to detect all the subtle flavors and to consider all its attributes.

I hope that this section will open up your eyes (and palate) to the many intricacies involved in detecting all these flavors and the delight of discovering new flavors in your cup.

It's your call

This invitation comes with a word of warning: This is an individual journey. Everyone perceives something different on their palate. What you find in the cup is perfectly valid.

Have you ever been to a wine tasting? Perhaps you've heard something like this said about a wine: "An elegant, focused wine with currant and floral herb aromas and appealing cherry, caramel and spice flavors." How do you react to that? All the flowery language can seem like downright snobbery. Perhaps you simply say, "It just tastes like wine to me."

However, people who taste wine repeatedly begin to note certain flavors. In order to describe them, they relate them to other food items they know well. So while the wine doesn't actually taste like caramel syrup, it does have sweet, warm, round notes that can be compared to caramel.

Something similar will happen in your journey with coffee. In the beginning you might say, "It just tastes like coffee to me." However, as you taste more, other flavors begin to come through.

The high notes of citrus fruits begin to thrill you. The warm notes of cacao comfort you. The nutty aftertaste satisfies you.

Welcome to the world of tasting specialty coffees. Have fun with it. Let your imagination run wild with the flavor sensations you detect.

Meeting the standards

The Specialty Coffee Association (SCA) has set specific standards for cupping coffee. Why? So that determining quality can standardized throughout the world.

When coffee is brewed, many variables affect the final outcome. As we'll discuss in Chapter 5, grind size, water temperature, coffee dose, and brew time (how long the water stays in contact with the coffee) all change the outcome.

To eliminate variations based on how coffee was prepared, the water and coffee for professional cupping sessions have to be exactly weighed, and the water has to be at a specific temperature. Additionally, the grinds should be left to brew for a specific amount of time.

Even the size of the cups is regulated. All the cups should hold the same amount of coffee, have the same dimensions, and be made of the same material.

According to the SCA, coffee should be roasted within 24 hours of the cupping session and the roast time is also pre-determined. The coffee should be ground just before cupping, so they'll probably grind it while you're watching.

Let's say you're going to participate in a coffee cupping in Bogota. You might be surprised by the amount of gadgets the baristas will use. A scale is essential, as well as a grinder, equipment to heat water to an exact temperature, and a cupping spoon to extract samples of the coffee.

Then you'll be ready to evaluate the brew.

Evaluating the brew

What does it mean to evaluate the brew? The idea is to evaluate the quality of the coffee. Now, this is where experience is important – drawing from past samples, a coffee cupper knows in what ways a certain coffee differs from others they've tasted.

Even if you're not an expert, you can still notice, identify, and describe what you experience. As you smell and taste your way through the samples, record your impressions.

By the end of the session your head will be filled with a whirlwind of flavors and opinions, and it can be hard to remember the details. That's why coffee cuppings are accompanied by forms and pencils.

Coffee is evaluated taking into account many attributes: fragrance, aroma, flavor, brightness (or acidity), sweetness, body, and more. In a professional cupping, each of these attributes receives a score. Let's explore each one in detail.

Fragrance/aroma

The first step is to evaluate fragrance and aroma. Fragrance and aroma are two words to define the same thing (the smell), but fragrance refers to dry coffee and aroma to the wet grinds.

Simply sniff the dry, freshly ground coffee. This is your first impression, your introduction to this coffee. It's like a handshake. The coffee is telling you who it is and what it does for a living. Listen to it.

After the grinds are infused with water, they are left for at least three minutes. You'll see a thick crust form over the top. Now comes one of the most exciting moments in the cupping – when the barista carefully breaks the crust with a spoon, releasing what is appropriately called the break aroma.

Feel free to sniff again. Now you can rate fragrance and aroma. Was it floral? Fruity? Herbal? Nutty? Chocolaty?

Slurp...

At this point you want to forget the aromas because you'll be moving on to the next – and most exciting – phase. Flavor.

Now the time has come for you to slurp your coffee. *What?* Didn't your mother teach you never to slurp? Well, sometimes it's necessary, and not just when you've got a hot bowl of soup in front of you.

You want to slurp your coffee in quickly enough so that it gets aerated and spreads all over your tongue and palate. That way your tongue can fully register the taste sensations. Also, your nose picks up on many aromas and helps you detect even more flavors.

So yes, we're telling you it is just fine to slurp the coffee – the louder the better – to get the full taste experience. Professional cuppers and baristas slurp long and loud, so don't be shy about your slurping.

Flavor

What flavors do you find in the coffee? As with most taste experiences, this is based on your personal opinion. You may find flavors common in coffee, such as berry or chocolate notes. Or you may feel your coffee tastes like a cinnamon bun with vanilla frosting. Or you may not find any of the flavors that others wax poetic about.

And frankly, if the coffee tastes like freshly cut summer grass to you, well...that's perfectly valid. Express what *you* find in the coffee.

Specialty coffees can cover a broad range of tastes. To help cuppers, the SCA dreamed up what they call the Flavor Wheel. This brightly colored wheel guides users to identify the tastes they find. The inner wheel has just a few notes, and from there the wheel branches out into thinner and thinner spokes with more possibilities.

So if you feel your coffee tastes fruity, this wheel helps you work through the flavor. Does that fruit taste like berries? Or does it lean more towards citrus, apple or cherry? If it tastes like berries, which one? Raspberry, blueberry or blackberry?

If it tastes like citrus – which is common in Colombia – do you get a lemony hint or an orange tanginess? Or perhaps lime? Or does your brew have a hint of tropical fruits like *lulo* or passion fruit?

As you can see, it is helpful to have the Flavor Wheel on hand when tasting specialty coffee. Of course, you may detect other flavors that are not on this wheel.

Certain flavors are common in Colombian coffees:

- **Floral**: hibiscus, jasmine blossoms, orange blossoms, lemongrass
- **Fruit**: grape, peach, apple, berry, black currant
- **Citrus**: lemon, orange, mandarin orange
- **Chocolate**: milk or dark chocolate
- **Sweet**: vanilla, honey, maple syrup, caramel, panela
- **Nut**: cashew, hazelnut, almond

Although you probably don't need to be told, scorched, skunky, sour, ashy or bitter coffee is bad. I hope you'll never taste coffees like that.

Now that the coffee has cooled a bit more it's at just the right temperature to taste again. When I first heard this, I said "I don't want cold coffee!" The reality is that for cupping, cooler coffee is better since you can detect more flavors. This is the moment to rate body, acidity, sweetness and balance, which we'll discuss now.

Body

Body is how the brew feels in your mouth – concentrate on how it rests on your tongue and the roof of your mouth.

Body can be heavy or light – and both can be pleasant. Colombian coffees tend to have medium body.

- Light: watery, tea-like
- Medium: smooth, syrupy, creamy
- Heavy: velvety, chewy, coating

Brightness or acidity

Brightness, or acidity, is important to coffee. This isn't the same type of acidity that may give you a sour stomach.

Brightness, or acidity, gives coffee a vibrant, crisp, lively taste. It is tangy and tart. It brings out the fruity and floral notes. Coffee that has no acidity is dull and muted and is frankly not worth drinking.

Take a slurp and concentrate on acidity. Does the coffee feel pleasantly bright? Is it refreshing, like the bite of a crisp apple?

Or is the brightness so intense it's unpleasant, like going too fast from a dark room out into a bright summer day? On the other hand, take note if it is too mild or if the coffee is flat (not a good thing in anything ranging from car tires to coffee).

Sweetness

As the coffee cools down more you can judge how sweet it is (as in not sour or astringent). Sweetness balances out acidity and makes for an exceptional cup – the more the better.

To help you understand the role of sweetness, imagine you're making lemonade. You start with tart juice and add water. Then you add sugar until the sweetness balances out the tartness. That's what sweetness should do for coffee; it eliminates any potential harshness.

Balance

Balance is simply how the above attributes all work together – flavor, body, acidity, and sweetness. You don't want any one attribute to overpower another. What you're looking for is complete harmony, like instruments in a finely tuned orchestra working together.

For instance, a heavy body would not work well with an insipid taste. It would be like drinking a full bodied red wine while dining on a delicate poached salmon. After sipping the heavy wine, you wouldn't be able to taste the salmon. The two just don't go together. Something similar happens if all the characteristics of coffee are not in balance.

Aftertaste or finish

The aftertaste is what lingers on your palate after you've swallowed the coffee. While first impressions are essential, aftertaste is critical. It's the feeling you'll be left with long after you've finished the coffee. It should last long enough (10-15 seconds) and should be refreshing, without defects.

As a special bonus, some coffees are so complex they change at the end. A fruity coffee may become nutty. Or a nutty coffee could have notes of chocolate at the end. A berry taste could yield to a full sweetness.

Clean Cup

The next characteristic to determine is how clean the cup is. Does that mean you should inspect to see if the barista washed the cup well? No, the phrase "clean cup" refers to a coffee that is free of defects.

What would defects be? For instance, did the coffee have an off flavor? Was it too light or too strong? Was it sour, fermented, rubbery? Those are all defects that would take away from the total score.

Overall

How did the coffee rate? Did it meet your expectations? Did it reflect the particular flavors common to the country or region it's from? This is your personal opinion, so express yourself!

Scoring

In a professional coffee cupping, each characteristic is given an individual score that is then calculated into a final score. This process is complex, and most coffee companies follow their own models.

What they all coincide in is that if the resulting number is below 80, it's not specialty coffee.

- Very good: 80-84.99
- Excellent: 85-89.99
- Outstanding: 90-100

Practice makes perfect

Of course, learning all of this takes time. A good way to practice is by attending coffee cuppings at specialty coffee shops. These are often offered free on a monthly basis and they're a great way to sharpen your skills.

After doing several coffee cuppings, sipping many coffees side by side, you can begin to distinguish one taste from another and understand the structure of each particular coffee. But in the end, all that matters is – was the coffee good? Was it great? And that is up to your individual taste.

If you want to organize a coffee tasting at home, it's simpler than it may seem. Choose two or three coffees with very different profiles. You want coffees that you can compare and contrast, not coffees that are too similar. If you want some suggestions, you can rely on your barista's recommendations to identify those coffees

Brew the coffee in the simplest way possible. If you want, brew it as the professional cuppers do – just put the coffee in a whiskey glass or a cup with a wide mouth and add water. When it has brewed, simply use a spoon to remove the coffee grinds that have floated to the top.

Use a fat soup spoon to sip one sample of the coffee (remember to slurp!). Stop to write down the flavors and other characteristics we've gone over in this chapter. Move on to the next sample. Slurp. Compare. Contrast.

It's more fun with friends, so invite a few buddies over to share the experience and give their opinions as to taste, body and brightness.

Remember that you want to record your impressions, since at the end of a cupping session all the tastes and special characteristics of the coffees can seem to blur together.

Impress the pros

The more you learn about specialty coffee, the more you'll enjoy drinking it. Tasting specialty coffee is much more complex than walking into a popular coffee chain store and ordering a double latte. Preparation and knowledge propel the experience beyond the basic and into the extraordinary.

Thus, knowledge makes you an insider in the immense, exciting, and ever-changing universe of specialty coffee.

After you obtain knowledge about specialty coffee – whether you get it from reading this book, taking a coffee tour, attending a coffee cupping, or participating in a roasting experience – you'll be anxious to visit your favorite coffee shop and put your newly acquired knowledge into practice.

Now you can walk into a specialty coffee shop and feel at home. Does the menu have a dizzying list of regions or countries, little-known coffee varieties, and strange-sounding processes and brewing methods? Those details can seem intimidating at first, but remember that you're now armed with facts and figures that few people know.

You'll be able to talk with the baristas about how the coffee was processed and the best brewing method for that particular coffee. You'll discover flavors like an experienced cupper. You'll discuss roasts and grinds just like the experts do.

In short, you'll be able to request your specialty coffee like a pro.

And you'll impress the baristas. *Please* impress the baristas. They'll love you for it.

After all, by showing you are fascinated with specialty coffee, you're validating the importance of their work. You're letting them know that their passion, their love, and their energy for coffee and what it means is not wasted on you. You value them and the work of every person who participated in the coffee chain. Even more, you're telling them you do believe that specialty coffee changes lives.

Meet the Experts

Tyler Youngblood is an American who was just passing through Colombia until he fell in love...with coffee.

He and his team at Azahar strive to make sure that the best coffee isn't simply shipped out of the country for others to enjoy. Their goal is to provide some of the best beans for Colombians who are just beginning to discover what superior coffee is all about.

Chapter 5

How to Brew Coffee

that Impresses your Barista

The secret is in the details

This is one of the most hands-on chapters of this book. This is where you'll learn about the brewing techniques that make specialty coffee...well, so special. You'll also get practical advice on how to make your home brew even better.

One comment I often hear about coffee is that the dry beans smell delicious and the aroma of a fresh brewed cup is tantalizing – but that the taste doesn't live up to the expectations. The reason can be the quality of the coffee beans themselves, but a lot also rests in the way coffee is brewed.

When you visit a specialty coffee shop you'll hear baristas discuss brewing methods. You'll see both simple brewing methods as well as visually stunning ones that look like science experiments.

At your favorite specialty coffee shop – here in Colombia or in your home country – you'll see baristas carefully prepare their tools to make a fantastic cup of coffee.

They weigh the coffee beans with a scale, then grind them to a specific point, and then heat and weigh the water (yes, they weigh both the water and the coffee). Then they bring together the water and the coffee grinds in a very specific pattern for a specific amount of time.

They're not just being fussy. These steps are important to get the most out of specialty coffee.

Of course, if you start with low quality coffee, it doesn't matter what your infusion time was, what temperature your water was at, or what kind of grinder you used. The results will be the same: an inferior cup.

However, specialty coffee can be coaxed to perfection using exacting procedures. And although you may not get the same results at home as that expert barista in your favorite coffee shop, you can still brew coffee you can be proud of. Brewing truly good coffee is a bit of work – but the results are sooooo worth it.

Where do you start?

Keep 'em fresh

Let's talk about the beans again. You want to start with the freshest beans possible. Why?

As beans sit around, they absorb moisture from the environment, and oxygen degrades bean quality. Then when you grind your coffee, the smaller particles are more exposed to air and degrade even faster.

Think about the last time you made fresh baked bread or bought it at the bakery – the bread tastes great the first day, but quickly goes stale. Within a week it is inedible.

Coffee also goes stale, so try to buy your beans freshly roasted in small quantities and grind just the amount you'll use right away.

Store them in an airtight container in a dry, dark, cool place, like a dungeon. Just kidding. A kitchen cabinet is just fine. You don't need to store them in your fridge or freezer, where they'll just pick up the flavors lurking in the forgotten corners.

Also, try to buy beans that have a clearly marked roasting date. Notice that I said roasting date and not some far-off expiration date. Ideally, you'll want to buy coffee within two weeks of roasting and only buy the amount you'll consume in a couple of weeks.

You also don't want to use coffee that is too freshly roasted. So if you happened to visit the roaster just as he's bagging a batch, let it rest for two to four days before brewing, and longer if you will make coffee with an espresso machine.

Back to the grind

I'm going to be completely frank with you. Anyone who buys specialty coffee really should invest in a grinder. I know it can seem so fussy to grind your beans every morning. I mean, does it really make that big of a difference?

Yes. It does. Get a grinder.

Remember what we said about stale bread? You don't want to be drinking stale beans. So after purchasing the fresh whole beans, grind 'em up just before using them.

Inexpensive blade grinders are available that do the job well enough. The blades do crush and grind the bean unevenly, however, and those uneven grinds could result in a bitter brew.

To get a consistent grind, a burr grinder is the one to do the job. Get an electric one if you're willing to splurge a bit. If you're grinding just for you, consider getting a less expensive and rather fun hand-cranked version.

Specialty coffee shops have industry grinders that are superior to what a person will typically have at home, so if you live close to one you may choose to grind your beans there.

The correct grind to use is determined mainly by the brewing method. It can seem complicated at first but it is simple once you learn. Since you probably only have one or two brewing methods at home, you only need to learn the grind for those methods.

The basic concept is that the longer the brewing time, the coarser the grind should be. Why?

Brewing finely ground coffee for a long period results will produce an over-extracted coffee, which is going to taste bitter. However, if you're making a cup using a short brewing time, coarse grinds won't extract enough and you'll wind up with a very weak brew.

So, if you're brewing in a French Press– which usually brews for 3-4 minutes – you need a coarser grind. An espresso, where the water is in contact with the coffee for just 20 seconds, requires a very fine grind.

However, feel free to experiment until you get to the perfect brew. For instance, if your coffee tastes flat, it may be under-extracted. Try using a finer grind. And if your coffee tastes bitter, it may be over-extracted. Go with a coarser grind the next time you make your brew.

Now, how do you know what is a fine grind versus a coarse grind? A fine grind will be roughly the size of table salt, while a medium grind will look more like kosher salt. A coarse grind has much larger, chunkier bits of coffee.

Are you ready for the numbers?

The heart of the matter is that coffee is quite picky about how it will release its flavors.

Think of an oyster that needs to be pried open. You treat it well, coax it gently, and you'll be rewarded. Coffee is very similar. How the water comes into contact with the coffee, as well as the amount of water and its temperature, has a big effect on the overall results. Just as you pry the oyster open, you want to pry the flavor from coffee.

To get the best brew, baristas use carefully calculated recipes. A word of warning to those who suffer from numerophobia: this involves math.

The coffee-to-water ratio usually falls somewhere between 15:1 and 17:1 (grams of water to grams of coffee). A good middle ground is 16:1.

If you're like me and you're allergic to numbers and ratios, you can calculate around 30-45 grams of coffee for about two cups of water. If you think more in terms of a cup of coffee, you'll want to use about 15-22 grams of coffee.

If those measurements are more than you want to get into before your first cup in the morning, 1½ to 2½ tablespoons of coffee is close enough (but please don't tell anyone I told you to use a tablespoon instead of a scale).

Now I'll throw in another complication and a warning. This ratio will vary depending on the specific coffee, the grind, the brewing method, and your own preference. For instance, a Chemex generally produces a lighter bodied brew, and therefore a 10:1 ratio is recommended (same amount of coffee, less water).

If all this measuring seems extreme to you, consider the last time you or a family member baked a cake. Did you pay attention to measurements? Yes, because you know that a slip-up will produce a flat cake or cookies that spread all over the pan. Similarly, baristas follow a recipe to ensure an optimum brew.

Now I'm going to hit you with another number: 195-205°F (about 90-96°C). That's how hot the water should be.

Why should water temperature matter to you? Water that's cooler won't extract the flavors of the coffee, and water that is too hot will produce an off-tasting brew.

If you have any doubts about the temperature, you can heat it to boiling and let it cool down a few degrees.

If you're in Bogota, forget about letting it cool down. While at sea level water boils at 212°F (100°C), at higher altitudes it boils at a lower temperature due to lower atmospheric pressure. So in Bogota water will be quite fine just off the boil.

Making the brew

So we've discussed beans, grind, water, and temperature. What's left? Oh yes, making the coffee. For this, you need your tools. So gather a timer, scale, stirrer, kettle, fresh water, and of course, the coffee.

It's time to make the brew.

Specialty coffee is fascinating to taste in any method, from espresso drinks to pour-over (manual) methods. Here we'll focus on how to make coffee in a pour-over method, which is easier to make at home since not everyone has an espresso machine on their kitchen counter.

For brewing methods that require a paper filter, pour a small amount of hot water over the filter, wetting it completely. You're going to want to do this for several reasons. First, it heats the brewer. It also seals the filter and eliminates any paper flavor.

Now dump out this initial water. Tare your kitchen scale to zero and weigh out the right amount of ground coffee according to your recipe.

Set your preferred brewing method on the scale and place the ground coffee in the filter. Hit tare again to set it at zero. Start your timer.

Now pour a small amount of water over the coffee just to cover it. Baristas prefer to use a narrow spout kettle to control water flow and direction. Allow the coffee to bloom (explained under the following subheading). The coffee will begin to release its aromas.

Wait about 30 seconds and pour the rest of the water slowly over the ground coffee, wetting all the grounds in a uniform way. A slow, continuous pour is better because the fresh water encourages extraction.

It takes a certain amount of time for coffee to release its positive flavors, and you want the coffee to have that quality time in the water. However, if you leave it too long in the water, it will begin to over-extract, or pull out bitter flavors that no one wants in their cup. So timing is important. Brew time should take between 3-5 minutes depending on the brewing method, which I'll explain in detail later in the chapter.

Pour yourself a cup of true specialty coffee made with your own hands. Now take a sip.

Wasn't it all worth it?

Time to bloom

I mentioned that coffee should be pre-infused for 30 seconds to allow it time to bloom. What does that mean?

When coffee is roasted, carbon dioxide builds up within the bean. It slowly creeps out after weeks, but with specialty coffees you're hopefully buying freshly roasted beans, which means it will still have a certain amount of carbon dioxide trapped inside. When you wet the coffee, the gas begins to escape (yes, coffee passes gas). You'll see the water bubbling up – in fact, with some roasts it's a way to judge just how fresh the coffee is.

The point is that while this gas is escaping, the water is having trouble getting in to extract the coffee. So you want to let the gas escape before completely wetting the coffee.

To illustrate this, imagine getting on a subway in a major city at rush hour. When the train comes to a stop in front of you, it's wise to wait until all the passengers flow out before you try to squeeze your way in.

With coffee, wait for the carbon dioxide to come out before you finish adding the water, which should only take 30 seconds. During this time you'll see the coffee bloom, or increase in size. Now it's ready for the rest of the water.

Is it true that experts recommend drinking pour-over coffees without milk or sugar?

Yes. In a world with few absolutes, one thing experts do agree on is that specialty coffee made in pour-over methods should be tasted without any additions. Which means no sugar. No cream. No milk.

That can be shocking to many coffee drinkers. Why would they recommend that? Do they want to torture you?

No torture is involved. The simple reason is that the experts want you to detect the flavor nuances, body, and other characteristics of these specialty coffees.

We've already talked about all the hard work that specialty coffee farmers have gone through to produce an exceptional coffee.

They selected the precise type of coffee tree for their farm. They harvested the coffee with best practices, processed it with painstaking attention to detail, and conscientiously transported it so that you get the best product possible.

Then, expert coffee roasters meticulously considered the best way to roast each batch. Coffee shop owners took measures to ensure that the coffee you drink is fresh. And the barista faithfully prepared the best brew for you.

Experts suggest you don't cover over all that hard work and mask the flavors inherent in those specialty coffees by adding additional ingredients. And I agree with them.

So taste your coffee bare and beautiful, just as the coffee farmer and roaster intended. Learn from the baristas about the flavors you can expect, and discover others they haven't told you about. Give the coffee a chance. However, if you feel you need sugar or sweeteners, they are available at the coffee shops.

Meet the Experts

Diego Campos has something to boast about. He has won the National Barista Championship several times. In fact, the year this book was written he was the current champion.

What are those championships like? It's like the Olympics, but caffeinated. Contestants train for months or years to perfect their barista skills, then compete in a series of judged competitions.

Stakes are high – winning can mean opportunities for work and travel. Diego has traveled throughout Europe, Asia and North America as an ambassador for Colombian coffee, and surely his passion will take him even farther.

Pour-over (manual) coffee brewing methods

Throughout this book I've mentioned that there are pour-over brewing methods, but what exactly does that mean?

Here I'll briefly describe some of the most common ones, all of which you'll see in specialty coffee shops around the world.

Chemex

If you think this coffee brewing method looks like a science experiment, you're right. Its design was inspired by a laboratory flask.

Developed in 1941 by the chemist Peter J. Schlumbohm, the Chemex is so well designed you can find it on display at the Museum of Modern Art in New York City, the Smithsonian in Washington D.C., and the Philadelphia Art Museum. The special filter retains oils and creates a distinctively clean taste experience. Use a medium grind and calculate a brew time between 3.5 and 4.5 minutes.

Aeropress

This unconventional brewing method was invented in the United States (2005) by engineer Alan Adler. Coffee (fine grind) is steeped and then forced through a paper or metal filter by pressing the plunger down through the tube. Benefits? It produces a full bodied coffee and it's fast. It's easy to travel with, so feel free to take it on your next camping trip.

The Aeropress is so popular among baristas that there are Aeropress Championships held around the world that award specially designed brewing methods as trophies. Use a medium-coarse grind and the total brewing time should be between 1.5-2 minutes.

French press

With no paper filter, the French press brews a strong coffee that captures the bean's flavor and oils. However, at times the brew can have a gritty feeling that is not to everyone's taste.

The French press is easy to use and is a no-brainer for the first cup of the morning – just push down the plunger and that's it. Remember to pour off any coffee you're not going to drink immediately to avoid over extraction and bitter tastes. Use a coarse grind and brew for 3-4 minutes.

V60 Dripper

The Japanese company Hario has created many designs, but coffee lovers are thankful for their V60 creation. The number comes from the angle of its cone (60 degrees). The cone shape ensures that the water maintains proper contact with the coffee.

The single hole in the bottom makes it easier to control brewing time; that means the barista can make a fuller bodied coffee or a lighter bodied one by pouring the water faster or slower.

You'll notice the ribbed design on the sides. That isn't just decoration; it allows air to escape and aids in extraction. This method produces balanced flavors with none of the bitterness and is good with floral, fruity coffees. Use a medium-fine grind and brew for less than 3 minutes.

Syphon

This coffee brewing method goes all the way back to the 1830s.

The name syphon comes from the ancient Greek word for "tube." It's also called a vacuum pot, which I don't like because it sounds like a household chore. It's actually a fun coffee brewing method, involving an open flame and a dramatic performance.

More akin to a physics experiment, this method is for science lovers. A flow of liquids is created when vapor pressure overcomes gravity and pushes water from the lower to upper chamber, where ground coffee is added.

After brewing, the flame or heating device is removed and the coffee descends to the bottom chamber, getting filtered along the way.

When done right, the Syphon produces a full bodied but clean brew. Done wrong, and it produces a burnt coffee. So you might want to leave this one to an expert barista. However, if you like the idea of having a chemistry set in your kitchen, be prepared to experiment quite a bit to get it right. Use a medium grind and lots of patience.

Your favorite brewing method

The brewing method you choose to use at home may be based on the taste profiles it brings out in a coffee. Or it could be based purely on convenience. Or economic considerations. Or the desire to impress family members and friends.

You can also choose to stock your kitchen with several methods that meet different needs.

Some people invest in an espresso maker. You may choose to use an electric drip brewer at home for your morning cup because it makes the amount of coffee you need to satisfy all the coffee drinkers in your family. You may choose a pour-over method for relaxed weekend mornings. Mix it up. That way you get the best out of every type of coffee.

I like intense coffees without much fuss, so I have a French press for my first coffee of the morning. However, my favorite method is Aeropress. It's a little more complex than the French Press (when I'm especially sleepy I have actually forgotten to put the filter in), so I only use it after I'm fully awake. My Chemex usually has its moment of stardom when guests visit, since I can make several cups at once and dazzle people with its beautiful form.

Tips you can apply in your kitchen

- Buy fresh roasted beans

- Grind them just before brewing

- Mind your numbers: use the appropriate coffee-
  to-water ratio

- Pay attention to water quality (think fresh and
  cool)

- Keep the water temperature just below boiling

- Pre-wet the filter

- Pre-infuse the coffee: wet the grinds and wait 30
  seconds

- Brewing time: let the coffee brew for the
  appropriate time for your method

10 Espresso Drinks Explained

You've probably heard about espresso, but you may not have tried it. It's a central part of the global specialty coffee scene. If you're in Bogota, be sure to try a variety of espresso drinks, since the brews are less expensive and the baristas are passionate about doing their best.

What is espresso?

In simple terms, espresso is made by forcing water at high pressure through finely ground coffee. The resulting drink is strong, small, and unforgettable.

Espresso is made with a machine that is conveniently called an espresso machine. That machine takes hot water (195-205° F or 92-95° C) and forces it at about 9 atmospheres of pressure through finely ground coffee for 20-30 seconds.

What in the world does that mean? Those 9 atmospheres of pressure are what they sounds like – it's nine times the atmospheric pressure. On planet earth. That's a lot of pressure, and it creates a creamy beverage unlike any other coffee-based drink.

Espresso should always be made to order with freshly ground coffee and consumed immediately. It's a small shot of coffee (just 25-35 ml), so don't expect a mug full of brew.

Using a shot of espresso as the base, there are a whole array of drinks that can be made. You're no doubt familiar with some, but others may have you scratching your head and asking, what is that?

Here's a helpful list that you can keep in mind when you sit down at a café and the waiter is gazing expectantly at you waiting for your order.

Americano

If you find an espresso too strong for you, try an americano. Two shots of espresso are topped off with hot water. In some cafés in Colombia, the waiter will just assume that an American (or any foreigner) is going to order an americano.

Cappuccino

One shot of espresso with equal parts of steamed milk and milk foam. The name of the drink refers to the color of the coffee when it gets its share of milk – it's similar to the brown robes Capuchin monks wear.

Latte

Simply the Italian word for milk, a latte will give you one shot of espresso with steamed milk. Foamed milk may also be added to the top. Beware that if you ask for a latte in Bogota, you may be served a cup of warm milk with just a touch of coffee. If I'm in the mood for a latte that actually tastes like coffee I'll ask for one with extra espresso.

Cortado

This version of espresso comes from Spain. One shot of espresso and equal parts hot milk make it small and powerful.

Doppio

Doppio (double) is simply a double espresso, or two shots.

Flat White

This drink from Australia (or New Zealand, depending on who's telling the story) has made its way to some Bogota coffee shops. Steamed milk is poured through and under two shots of espresso, resulting in a drink with no foam (thus flat) and whiter than most other espresso based drinks.

Macchiato

Macchiato, which means stained, is one shot of espresso that is 'stained' with a small portion of textured milk or foam.

Ristretto

Ristretto, or 'restricted' coffee, is an espresso made using the same amount of ground coffee but less water in a bitter, intense brew.

Affogato

This drink means 'drowned'. In ice cream, that is. It's a dessert that you'll see around Bogota, espresso with ice cream.

Colombia's secret world

As I've mentioned, the coffee chain doesn't end when the coffee bags show up at a coffee shop. That is the moment when the torch is simply passed on to another team member.

It took me some time to fully realize the importance of the last player in this chain of coffee production. In fact, I spent enormous amounts of time drinking many cups of coffee with Bogota's enthusiastic coffee shop owners and talented and generous baristas before I realized I'd found something amazing.

In this megacity that embraces eight million people I had found a hidden world: Bogota's specialty coffee scene.

This coffee scene is not purposely hidden from sight. It is actually right out in the open, but it is so complex and nuanced that people can enter and exit coffee shops for years without recognizing it.

Because it's easy to focus on the coffee and forget about the hands that prepared it.

What makes this scene so amazing is not just the coffee. It isn't all those fascinating brewing methods, either. It's not just the cute shops with on-site coffee labs, comfortable sofas, and free WiFi.

Yes, Bogota has something extremely precious that you might not notice at first. The baristas.

These baristas love what they do. They live to share their fascination with true specialty coffee. Working closely with these young Colombian men and women, I have to admit I've fallen in love with them.

Over months and years of training and work, careful baristas cultivate a perfectionist mentality. Their movements become precise, their understanding of varieties and roasts and temperatures deepens.

Without the knowledge they apply to each coffee, the brew would simply be a mediocre hot drink handed over the counter to the customer. With dedication and care, a dedicated barista hands over centuries of coffee culture to each customer they serve.

They are enthusiastic, dedicated, cheerful, and hard-working. They make the coffee scene in Bogota extraordinary. Their devotion to coffee, to the flavors and characteristics and changing variables in each batch of specialty coffee, is outstanding.

I have toured coffee shops and roasters in the United States, where I met dedicated baristas and roasters. But Colombians take dedication to a level of intensity I have rarely seen elsewhere. It's imprinted on their cultural fiber. They do what they do with a sense of presence, immediacy and engagement that I have never seen in any other country I've visited.

Naturally, it is not only the baristas who have that passion – hang around the country during an important soccer match and you'll see it, hear it, and feel it. The roaring intensity will sweep you away.

Now imagine that presence, immediacy, and engagement hyped up on some serious caffeine levels and you can understand why these baristas are unforgettable.

Naturally, the baristas are not the only passionate ones. An ever-growing number of coffee shop owners don't view a coffee shop as just a business. It's not even just a way of life. It's a way of changing lives, providing new opportunities, shaping culture, and impacting the future of an entire country.

Each time you purchase a bag of specialty coffee in Colombia, you're adding to that dream of a better life now and a brighter future for the many families that depend on coffee.

All along the coffee chain, which is a series of tightly interconnected links, people benefit from the added value of specialty coffee.

Farmers receive better prices for their coffee. Skilled roasters earn a living practicing a craft they love. Baristas gain a profession they're proud of, even if they couldn't afford the luxury of a university degree.

Specialty coffee is changing lives all over the world.

Be a part of the change.

How can you have memorable coffee experiences?

You could do what I did – hang out for endless hours at coffee shops around the city. Make friends with the baristas. Try their lattes and espressos and pour-overs. Talk with them about roasts and processes and grinds. Soak up their knowledge so you can grasp the full meaning of specialty coffee.

Naturally, that takes time. If you're on a tighter schedule, you can have that knowledge handed to you in a more concentrated form.

You could participate in a coffee tasting at a local coffee shop. Or you could take a coffee shop tour where you can learn about coffee history and culture, where you'll be introduced to the baristas and you can listen to their stories.

If you have a full day, visit a coffee farm to see where it all begins and how an apparently tasteless seed becomes a coveted beverage. If you have even more time, you could take a cupping certification or even go through a whole barista course.

All of these activities give you the key to continue the legacy of passion, dedication, and fascination with coffee that starts with the farmer, is passed on through the roaster, and is handed to you by the barista.

In this book you've learned about coffee from its remote origins and how it has traveled around the world. You now understand the basics of how it's grown, how it's transformed and how it reaches you. You know which brewing method to choose, how to use it, and how to get the best results at home.

I've given you the tools to understand coffee on a deeper level, love it for all its complexities and surprises, taste it like a pro, and brew it with confidence.

So, yes, go ahead and slurp. You have my permission.

Thank you for reading
Permission to Slurp

If you enjoyed this guide to tasting coffee in Colombia, please take a few minutes to leave a review on Amazon. Reviews help other coffee lovers know if the book is right for them.

Of course, it also helps me! One of the ways it helps is to know what you loved, what you didn't, and what you'd like to read about in future books.

Thanks in advance!

About the Author - Karen Attman

Over twenty years ago I left my hometown of Philadelphia to pursue expat life. When I moved to Bogota, Colombia, I started Flavors of Bogota, an online magazine that examines food and drink around Colombia.

It didn't take me long to fall in love with the coffee culture I found in Colombia. I created the Flavors of Bogota Specialty Coffee Experiences to introduce people to the marvels of Colombia's specialty coffee scene.

I do think – and write – about things besides coffee. I have written about food, travel and business for over 20 publications around the world, including books, newspapers, magazines and websites. Perhaps you've seen my work in CNN, Esquire, Four Magazine, and National Geographic.

Write to me at karen (at) flavorsofbogota.com. I'd love to answer any questions you have about coffee in Colombia.

And please keep an eye out for upcoming books about my Colombian coffee journey.

About Flavors of Bogota

Flavors of Bogota, Colombia's top English-language online food magazine, is on a never-ending coffee and food adventure.

We highlight exceptional baristas, talented roasters, coffee shop owners that are making a difference, and hard-working coffee growers whose lives are improved through specialty coffee. We also explore the restaurant scene, street foods, and Latin American ingredients that you'll want to try out in your own kitchen.

Come along with us on our journey! Check out our online magazine at FlavorsofBogota.com. We also talk about the food scene in Colombia on social media, so we invite you to join us on Facebook, Instagram, Twitter, and Pinterest – you'll find us when you search for FlavorsofBogota.

Flavors of Bogota Specialty Coffee Experiences

If you live in Colombia or will visit soon, join us for a Specialty Coffee Experience.

Our experiences are an adventure in the flavors, aromas and heartwarming stories about coffee. We'll introduce you to the best coffees in Bogota, the complex world of specialty coffee, and the people who make it all happen.

Acknowledgments

Producing a book is a community effort. Just as it takes a whole village to raise a child, it takes a community to finish a book and launch it out into the world. And while there's not enough room here to thank every person who contributed to making this book possible, I'll give you the short list.

Thanks to the first entrepreneur to show me what determination, perseverance, and hard work can achieve: my mother.

Thanks to every coffee expert who has guided me since I began learning about specialty coffee. Getting a coffee education in Colombia is easy because of the generosity and enthusiasm of so many spectacular baristas, coffee shop owners and managers, and dedicated roasters.

There isn't room to list every expert, but a few that shaped my journey are: Alejandra Ramos (my partner in coffee crime), Luis Fernando Vélez, Manuel Barbosa., Diego Campos, Sebastian Hernandez, Jasmin Lesmes, Steven Martinez, Manuel Torres, and Stephany and Alex Moore.

Tom Le Mesurier from EatRio started me on the road to teaching others about food and drink in Latin America. A conversation we had in Mexico City opened up whole new possibilities. Thanks, Tom; I owe you a drink when we meet again.

Thanks to my coach, Emily Maher – her excitement for the creative process and her gentle touch guided me to create my best work.

Thanks to Emma Newbery, owner and editor-in-chief of The Bogota Post, for her constant encouragement as well as her keen vision and superb editing skills.

Rayna Bolich, Marcela Merrifield, and Cristie Valencia were kind enough to go through the first draft of this manuscript and tell me what worked for them and what didn't. I owe you all a cup of coffee – and much more!

The Bogota International Press provided invaluable publishing services that helped this book on its path to publication.

I also have to mention the patience of my husband, who quietly endured the long hours I spent shut away in the office preparing this manuscript.

And my special gratitude goes to Victoria Kellaway, the talented author behind *Colombia a Comedy of Errors* and Banana Skin Flip Flops, for her creativity, unflagging enthusiasm, and eye for detail.

For anyone whose name is not listed here, know that I appreciated your help and guidance in the coffee and book publishing journey that produced *Permission to Slurp*. Thank you.

If you'll be visiting Bogota and need a list of specialty coffee shops to visit, download the Quick Guide to Specialty Coffee Shops on Flavors of Bogota.

The Quick Guide is free! Just go to FlavorsofBogota.com to download it.